Some Notes on River Country

Eudora Welty

Some Notes on River Country

ILLUSTRATED WITH TWENTY-EIGHT OF HER PHOTOGRAPHS

AFTERWORD BY HUNTER COLE

University Press of Mississippi

A Mary Jayne G. Whittington Book in the Arts

www.upress.state.ms.us

The University Press of Mississippi is a member

of the Association of American University Presses.

Manufactured in Canada

ISBN 1-57806-525-9

05 04 03   4 3 2 1

Photographs on pages 2, 52, and 57 are by Frank H. Lyell, courtesy of Louis J. Lyell

Some Notes on River Country

Ruins of Windsor / NEAR PORT GIBSON

A PLACE that ever was lived in is like a fire that never goes out. It flares up, it smolders for a time, it is fanned or smothered by circumstance, but its being is intact, forever fluttering within it, the result of some original ignition. Sometimes it gives out glory, sometimes its little light must be sought out to be seen, small and tender as a candle flame, but as certain.

I have never seen, in this small section of old Mississippi River country and its little chain of lost towns between Vicksburg and Natchez, anything so mundane as ghosts, but I have felt many times there a sense of place as powerful as if it were visible and walking and could touch me.

The clatter of hoofs and the bellow of boats have gone, all old communications. The Old Natchez Trace has sunk out of use; it is deep in leaves. The river has gone away and left the landings. Boats from Liverpool do not dock at these empty crags. The old deeds are done, old evil and old good have been made into stories, as plows turn up the river bottom, and the wild birds fly now at the level where people on boat deck once were strolling and talking of great expanding things, and of chance and money. Much beauty has gone, many little things of life. To light up the nights there are no mansions, no celebrations. Just as, when there were mansions and celebrations, there were no more festivals of an Indian tribe there; before the music, there were drums.

But life does not forsake any place. People live still in Rodney's Landing; flood drives them out and they return to it. Children are born there and find the day as inexhaustible and as abundant as they run and wander in their little hills as they, in innocence and rightness, would find it anywhere on earth. The seasons come as truly, and give gratefulness, though they bring little fruit. There is a sense of place there, to keep life from being extinguished, like a cup of the hands to hold a flame.

To go there, you start west from Port Gibson. This was the frontier of the Natchez country. Postmen would arrive here blowing their tin horns like Gabriel where the Old Natchez Trace crosses the Bayou Pierre, after riding three hundred wilderness miles from Tennessee, and would run in where the tavern used to be to deliver their mail, change their ponies, and warm their souls with grog. And up this now sand-barred bayou trading vessels would ply from the river. Port Gibson is on a highway and a railroad today, and lives on without its river life, though it is half diminished. It is still rather smug because General Grant said it was "too pretty to burn." Perhaps it was too pretty for any harsh fate, with its great mossy trees and old camellias, its exquisite little churches, and galleried houses back in the hills overlooking the cotton fields. It has escaped what happened to Grand Gulf and Bruinsburg and Rodney's Landing.

A narrow gravel road goes into the West. You have entered the loess country, and a gate might have been shut behind you for the difference in the world. All about are hills and chasms of cane, forests of cedar trees, and magnolia. Falling away from your road, at times merging with it, an old trail crosses and recrosses, like a tunnel through the dense brakes, under arches of branches, a narrow, cedar-smelling trace the width of a horseman. This road joined the Natchez Trace to the river. It, too, was made by buffaloes, then used by man, trodden lower and lower, a few inches every hundred years.

Loess has the beautiful definition of aeolian—wind-borne. The loess soil is like a mantle; the ridge was laid down here by the wind, the bottom land by the water. Deep under them both is solid blue clay, embalming the fossil horse and fossil ox and the great mastodon, the same preserving blue clay that was dug up to wrap the head of the Big Harp in bandit days, no less a monstrous thing when it was carried in for reward.

Loess exists also in China, that land whose plants are so congenial to the South; there the bluffs rise vertically for five hundred feet in some places and contain cave dwellings without number. The Mississippi bluffs once served the same purpose; when Vicksburg was being shelled from the river during the year's siege there in the War Between the States, it was the daily habit of the three thousand women, children and old men who made up the wartime population to go on their all-fours into shelters they had tunneled into the loess bluffs. Mark Twain reports how the Federal soldiers would shout from the river in grim humor, "Rats, to your holes!"

Winding through this land unwarned, rounding to a valley, you will come on a startling thing. Set back in an old gray field, with horses grazing like small fairy animals beside it, is a vast ruin—twenty-two Corinthian columns in an empty oblong and an L. Almost seeming to float like lace, bits of wrought-iron balcony connect them here and there. Live cedar trees are growing from the iron black acanthus leaves, high in the empty air. This is the ruin of Windsor, long since burned. It used to have five stories and an observation tower—Mark Twain used the tower as a sight when he was pilot on the river.

Immediately the cane and the cedars become more impenetrable, the road ascends and descends, and rather slowly, because of the trees and the shadows, you realize a little village is before you. Grand Gulf today looks like a scene in Haiti. Under enormous dense trees where the moss hangs long as ladders, there are hutlike buildings and pale whitewashed sheds; most of the faces under the straw hats are black, and only narrow jungly paths lead toward the river. Of course this is not Grand Gulf in the original, for the river undermined that and pulled it whole into the river—the opposite of what it did to Rodney's Landing. A little corner was left, which the Federals burned, all but a wall, on their way to Vicksburg. After the war the population built it back—and the river moved away. Grand Gulf was a British settlement before the Revolution and had close connection with England, whose ships traded here. It handled more cotton than any other port in Mississippi for about twenty years. The old cemetery is there still, like a roof of marble and moss overhanging the town and about to tip into it. Many names of British gentry stare out from the stones, and the biggest snakes in the world must have their kingdom in the dark-green tangle.

Two miles beyond, at the end of a dim jungle track where you can walk, is the river, immensely wide and vacant, its bluff occupied sometimes by a casual camp of fishermen under the willow trees, where dirty children play-ing about and nets drying have a look of timeless roaming and poverty and sameness. . . . By boat you can reach a permanent fishing camp, inaccessible now by land. Go till you find the hazy shore where the Bayou Pierre, divid-ing in two, reaches around the swamp to meet the river. It is a gray-green land, softly flowered, hung with stillness. Houseboats will be tied there among the cypresses under falls of long moss, all of a color. Aaron Burr's "flotilla" tied up there, too, for this is Bruinsburg Landing, where the boats were seized one wild day of apprehension. Bruinsburg grew to be a rich, gay place in cotton days. It is almost as if a wand had turned a noisy cotton port into a handful of shanty boats. Yet Bruinsburg Landing has not vanished: it is this.

Wonderful things have come down the current of this river, and more spectacular things were on the water than could ever have sprung up on shores then. Every kind of treasure, every kind of bearer of treasure has come down, and armadas and flotillas, and the most frivolous of things, too, and the most pleasure-giving of people.

Natchez, downstream, had a regular season of drama from 1806 on, attended by the countryside—the only one in English in this part of the world. The plays would be given outdoors, on a strip of grass on the edge of the high bluff overlooking the landing. With the backdrop of the river and the endless low marsh of Louisiana beyond, some version of Elizabethan or Restoration comedy or tragedy would be given, followed by a short farcical afterpiece, and the traveling company would run through a little bird mimicry, ventriloquism and magical tricks in-between. Natchez, until lately a bear-baiting crowd, watched eagerly "A Laughable Comedy in 3 Acts written by Shakespeare and Altered by Garrick called Catherine & Petrucio," followed by "A Pantomime Ballet Called a Trip through the Vauxhall Gardens into which is introduced the humorous song of Four and Twenty Fiddlers concluding with a dance by the characters." Or sometimes the troupe would arrive with a program of "divertisements"—recitations of Lochinvar, Alexander's Feast, Cato's Soliloquy of the Soul, and Clarence's Dream, interspersed with Irish songs by the boys sung to popular requests and concluding with "A Laughable Combat between Two Blind Fiddlers."

The Natchez country took all this omnivorously to its heart. There were rousing, splendid seasons, with a critic writing pieces in the newspaper to say that last night's Juliet spoke just a *bit* too loudly for a girl, though Tybalt kept in perfect character to delight all, even after he was dead—signed "X.Y.Z."

But when the natural vigor of the day gave clamorous birth to the minstrel show, the bastard Shakespeare went; and when the showboat really rounded the bend, the theatre of that day, a child of the plantation and the river, came to its own. The next generation heard calliopes filling river and field with their sound, and saw the dazzling showboats come like enormous dreams up the bayous and the little streams at floodtime, with whole French Zouave troops aboard, whole circuses with horses jumping through paper hoops, and all the literal rites of the minstrel show, as ever true to expectations as a miracle play.

Now if you pick up the Rodney Road again, through twenty miles of wooded hills, you wind sharply round, the old sunken road ahead of you and following you. Then from a great height you descend suddenly through a rush of vines, down, down, deep into complete levelness, and there in a strip at the bluff's foot, at the road's end, is Rodney's Landing.

Though you walk through Rodney's Landing, it long remains a landscape, rather than a center of activity, and seems to exist altogether in the sight, like a vision. At first you think there is not even sound. The thick soft morning shadow of the bluff on the valley floor, and the rose-red color of the brick church which rises from this shadow, are its dominant notes—all else seems green. The red of the bricks defies their element; they were made of earth, but they glow as if to remind you that there is fire in earth. No one is in sight.

Eventually you see people, of course. Women have little errands, and the old men play checkers at a table in front of the one open store. And the people's faces are good. Theirs seem *actually* the faces your eyes look for in city streets and never see. There is a middle-aged man who always meets you when you come. He is like an embodiment of the simplicity and friendliness not of the mind—for his could not teach him—but of the open spirit. He never remembers you, but he speaks courteously. "I am Mr. John David's boy—where have you come from, and when will you have to go back?" He has what I have always imagined as a true Saxon face, like a shepherd boy's, light and shy and set in solitude. He carries a staff, too, and stands with it on the hill, where he will lead you—looking with care everywhere and far away, warning you of the steep stile. . . . The river is not even in sight here. It is three miles beyond, past the cotton fields of the bottom, through a dense miasma of swamp.

The houses merge into a shaggy fringe at the foot of the bluff. It is like a town some avenging angel has flown over, taking up every second or third house and leaving only this. There are more churches than houses now; the edge of town is marked by a little wooden Catholic church tiny as a match-box, with twin steeples carved like icing, over a stile in a flowery pasture. The Negro Baptist church, weathered black with a snow-white door, has red hens in the yard. The old galleried stores are boarded up. The missing houses were burned—they were empty, and the little row of Negro inhabitants have carried them off for firewood.

You know instinctively as you stand here that this shelf of forest is the old town site, and you find that here, as in Grand Gulf, the cemetery has remained as the roof of the town. In a mossy wood the graves, gently tended here, send up mossy shafts, with lilies flowering in the gloom. Many of the tombstones are marked "A Native of Ireland," though there are German names and graves neatly bordered with sea shells and planted in spring-flowering bulbs. People in Rodney's Landing won silver prizes in the fairs for their horses; they planted all this land; some of them were killed in battle, some in duels fought on a Grand Gulf sand bar. The girls who died young of the fevers were some of the famous "Rodney heiresses." All Mississippians know descendants of all the names. I looked for the grave of Dr. Nutt, the man who privately invented and used his cotton gin here, previous to the rest of the world. The Petit Gulf cotton was known in England better than any other as superior to all cotton, and was named for the little gulf in the river at this landing, and Rodney, too, was once called Petit Gulf.

Down below, Mr. John David's boy opens the wrought-iron gate to the churchyard of the rose-red church, and you go up the worn, concave steps. The door is never locked, the old silver knob is always the heat of the hand. It is a church, upon whose calm interior nothing seems to press from the outer world, which, though calm itself here, is still "outer." (Even cannonballs were stopped by its strong walls, and are in them yet.) It is the kind of little church in which you might instinctively say prayers for your friends; how is it that both danger and succor, both need and response, seem intimately near in little country churches?

Something always hangs imminent above all life—usually claims of daily need, daily action, a prescribed course of movement, a schedule of time. In Rodney, the imminent thing is a natural danger—the town may be flooded by the river, and every inhabitant must take to the hills. Every house wears a belt of ineradicable silt around its upper walls. I asked the storekeeper what his store would be like after the river had been over it, and he said, "You know the way a fish is?" Life threatened by nature is simplified, most peaceful in present peace, quiet in seasons of waiting and readiness. There are rowboats under all the houses.

Even the women in sunbonnets disappear and nothing moves at noon but butterflies, little white ones, large black ones, and they are like some flutter of heat, some dervishes of the midday hour, as in pairs they rotate about one another, ascending and descending, appearing to follow each other up and down some swaying spiral staircase invisible in the dense light. The heat moves. Its ripples can be seen, like the ripples in some vertical river running between earth and sky. It is so still at noon. I was never there before the river left, to hear the thousand swirling sounds it made for Rodney's Landing, but could it be that its absence is so much missed in the life of sound here that a stranger would feel it? The stillness seems absolute, as the brightness of noon seems to touch the point of saturation. Here the noon sun does make a trance; here indeed at its same zenith it looked down on life sacrificed to it and was worshipped.

It is not strange to think that a unique nation among Indians lived in this beautiful country. The origin of the Natchez is still in mystery. But their people, five villages in the seventeenth century, were unique in this country and they were envied by the other younger nations—the Choctaws helped the French in their final dissolution. In Mississippi they were remnants surely of medievalism. They were proud and cruel, gentle-mannered and ironic, handsome, extremely tall, intellectual, elegant, pacific and ruthless. Fire, death, sacrifice formed the spirit of the Natchez' worship. They did not now, however, make war.

The women—although all the power was in their blood, and a Sun woman by rigid system married a low-caste Stinkard and bore a Sun child by him—were the nation's laborers still. They planted and they spun, they baked their red jugs for the bear oil, and when the men came from the forests, they would throw at the feet of their wives the tongues of the beasts they had shot from their acacia bows—both as a tribute to womanhood and as a command to the wives to go out and hunt on the ground for what they had killed, and to drag it home.

The town of Natchez was named after this nation, although the French one day, in a massacre for a massacre, slew or sent into slavery at Santo Domingo every one of its namesakes, and the history of the nation was done in 1773. The French amusedly regarded the Natchez as either *"sauvages"* or *"naturels, innocents."* They made many notes of their dress and quaint habits, made engravings of them looking like Cupids and Psyches, and handed down to us their rites and customs with horrified withholdings or fascinated repetitions. The women fastened their knee-length hair in a net of mulberry threads, men singed theirs short into a crown except for a lock over the left ear. They loved vermilion and used it delicately, men and women, the women's breasts decorated in tattooed designs by whose geometrics they strangely match ancient Aztec bowls. *"En été"* male and female wore a draped garment from waist to knee. *"En hyver"* they threw about them swan-feather mantles, made as carefully as wigs. For the monthly festivals the men added bracelets of skin polished like ivory, and thin disks of feathers went in each hand. They were painted fire-color, white puffs of down decorated their shorn heads, the one lock left to support the whitest feathers. As children, the Natchez wore pearls handed down by their ancestors—pearls which they had ruined by piercing them with fire.

The Natchez also laughed gently at the French. (Also they massacred them when they were betrayed by them.) Once a Frenchman asked a Natchez noble why these Indians would laugh at them, and the noble replied that it was only because the French were like geese when they talked—all clamoring at once. The Natchez never spoke except one at a time; no one was ever interrupted or contradicted; a visitor was always allowed the opening speech, and that after a rest in silence of fifteen or twenty minutes, to allow him to get his breath and collect his thoughts. (Women murmured or whispered; their game after labor was a silent little guessing game played with three sticks that could not disturb anyone.) But this same nation, when any Sun died, strangled his wife and a great company of loyal friends and ambitious Stinkards to attend him in death, and walked bearing his body over the bodies of strangled infants laid before him by their parents. A Sun once expressed great though polite astonishment that a certain Frenchman declined the favor of dying with him.

Their own sacrifices were great among them. When Iberville came, the Natchez had diminished to twelve hundred. They laid it to the fact that the fire had once been allowed to go out and that a profane fire burned now in its place. Perhaps they had prescience of their end—the only bit of their history that we really know.

Today Rodney's Landing wears the cloak of vegetation which has caught up this whole land for the third time, or the fourth, or the hundredth. There is something Gothic about the vines, in their structure in the trees—there are arches, flying buttresses, towers of vines, with trumpet flowers swinging in them for bells and staining their walls. And there is something of a warmer grandeur in their very abundance—stairways and terraces and whole hanging gardens of green and flowering vines, with a Babylonian babel of hundreds of creature voices that make up the silence of Rodney's Landing. Here are nests for birds and thrones for owls and trapezes for snakes, every kind of bower in the world. From earliest spring there is something, when garlands of yellow jasmine swing from tree to tree, in the woods aglow with dogwood and redbud, when the green is only a floating veil in the hills.

And the vines make an endless flourish in summer and fall. There are wild vines of the grape family, with their lilac and turquoise fruits and their green, pink and white leaves. Muscadine vines along the stream banks grow a hundred feet high, mixing their dull, musky, delicious grapes among the bronze grapes of the scuppernong. All creepers with trumpets and panicles of scarlet and yellow cling to the treetops. On shady stream banks hang lady's eardrops, fruits and flowers dangling pale jade. The passionflower puts its tendrils where it can, its strange flowers of lilac rays with their little white towers shining out, or its fruit, the maypop, hanging. Wild wistaria hangs its flowers like flower-grapes above reach, and the sweetness of clematis, the virgin's-bower which grows in Rodney, and of honeysuckle, must fill even the highest air. There is a vine that grows to great heights, with heart-shaped leaves as big and soft as summer hats, overlapping and shading everything to deepest jungle blue-green.

Ferns are the hidden floor of the forest, and they grow, too, in the trees, their roots in the deep of mossy branches.

All over the hills the beautiful white Cherokee rose trails its glossy dark-green leaves and its delicate luminous-white flowers. Foliage and flowers alike have a quality of light and dark as well as color in Southern sun, and sometimes a seeming motion like dancing due to the flicker of heat, and are luminous or opaque according to the time of day or the density of summer air. In early morning or in the light of evening they become translucent and ethereal, but at noon they blaze or darken opaquely, and the same flower may seem sultry or delicate in its being all according to when you see it.

It is not hard to follow one of the leapings of old John Law's mind, then, and remember how he displayed diamonds in the shop windows in France—during the organization of his Compagnie d'Occident—saying that they were produced in the cups of the wildflowers along the lower Mississippi. And the closer they grew to the river, the more nearly that might be true.

Deep in the swamps the water hyacinths make solid floors you could walk on over still black water, the Southern blue flag stands thick and sweet in the marsh. Lady's-tresses, greenish-white little orchids with spiral flowers and stems twisted like curls and braids, grow there, and so do nodding lady's-tresses. Water lilies float, and spider lilies rise up like little coral monsters.

The woods on the bluffs are the hardwood trees—dark and berried and flowered. The magnolia is the spectacular one with its heavy cups—they look as heavy as silver—weighing upon its aromatic, elliptical, black-green leaves, or when it bears its dense pink cones. I remember an old botany book, written long ago in England, reporting the magnolia by hearsay, as having blossoms "so large as to be distinctly visible a mile or more—seen in the mass, we presume." But I tested the visibility power of the magnolia, and the single flower can be seen for several miles on a clear day. One magnolia cousin, the cucumber tree, has long sleevelike leaves and pale-green flowers which smell strange and cooler than the grandiflora flower. Set here and there in this country will be a mimosa tree, with its smell in the rain like a cool melon cut, its puffs of pale flowers settled in its sensitive leaves.

Perhaps the live oaks are the most wonderful trees in this land. Their great girth and their great spread give far more feeling of history than any house or ruin left by man. Vast, very dark, proportioned as beautifully as a church, they stand majestically in the wild or line old sites, old academy grounds. The live oaks under which Aaron Burr was tried at Washington, Mississippi, in this section, must have been old and impressive then, to have been chosen for such a drama. Spanish moss invariably hangs from the live oak branches, moving with the wind and swaying its long beards, darkening the forests; it is an aerial plant and strangely enough is really a pineapple, and consists of very, very tiny leaves and flowers, springy and dustily fragrant to the touch; no child who has ever "dressed up" in it can forget the sweet dust of its smell. It would be hard to think of things that happened here without the presence of these live oaks, so old, so expansive, so wonderful, that they might be sentient beings. W. H. Hudson, in his autobiography, *Far Away and Long Ago*, tells of an old man who felt reverentially toward the ancient trees of his great country house, so that each night he walked around his park to visit them one by one, and rest his hand on its bark to bid it good-night, for he believed in their knowing spirits.

Now and then comes a report that an ivory-billed woodpecker is seen here. Audubon in his diary says the Indians began the slaughter of this bird long before Columbus discovered America, for the Southern Indians would trade them to the Canadian Indians—four buckskins for an ivory bill. Audubon studied the woodpecker here when he was in the Natchez country, where it lived in the deepest mossy swamps along the windings of the river, and he called it "the greatest of all our American woodpeckers and probably the finest in the world." The advance of agriculture rather than slaughter has really driven it to death, for it will not live except in a wild country.

This woodpecker used to cross the river "in deep undulations." Its notes were "clear, loud, and rather plaintive . . . heard at a considerable distance . . . and resemble the false high note of a clarinet." "Pait, pait, pait," Audubon translates it into his Frenchlike sound. It made its nest in a hole dug with the ivory bill in a tree inclined in just a certain way—usually a black cherry. The holes went sometimes three feet deep, and some people thought they went spirally. The bird ate the grapes of the swampland. Audubon says it would hang by its claws like a titmouse on a grapevine and devour grapes by the bunch—which sounds curiously as though it knew it would be extinct before very long. This woodpecker also would destroy any dead tree it saw standing—chipping it away "to an extent of twenty or thirty feet in a few hours, leaping downward with its body . . . tossing its head to the right and left, or leaning it against the bark to ascertain the precise spot where the grubs were concealed, and immediately renewing its blows with fresh vigor, all the while sounding its loud notes, as if highly delighted." The males had beautiful crimson crests, the females were "always the most clamorous and the least shy." When caught, the birds would fight bitterly, and "utter a mournful and very piteous cry." All vanished now from the earth—the piteous cry and all; unless where Rodney's swamps are wild enough still, perhaps it is true, the last of the ivory-billed woodpeckers still exist in the world, in this safe spot, inaccessible to man.

Indians, Mike Fink the flatboatman, Burr, and Blennerhassett, John James Audubon, the bandits of the Trace, planters, and preachers—the horse fairs, the great fires—the battles of war, the arrivals of foreign ships, and the coming of floods: could not all these things still move with their true stature into the mind here, and their beauty still work upon the heart? Perhaps it is the sense of place that gives us the belief that passionate things, in some essence, endure. Whatever is significant and whatever is tragic in its story live as long as the place does, though they are unseen, and the new life will be built upon these things—regardless of commerce and the way of rivers and roads, and other vagrancies.

The Mississippi / NEAR VICKSBURG

Ghost river town / RODNEY

Home / NEAR NATCHEZ TRACE

Baptist church / RODNEY

Cemetery / RODNEY

Cemetery / RODNEY

Catholic church / RODNEY

Tomb with top ajar / RODNEY

Church Hill / NEAR OLD WASHINGTON

Cemetery stile / RODNEY

Cemetery / NATCHEZ TRACE AREA

Home, ghost river town / RODNEY

Hamlet / RODNEY

Cemetery / RODNEY

Bethel church / NEAR RODNEY

Hanging nets / NEAR GRAND GULF

Hamlet / RODNEY

Fisherman and his boys throwing knives at a target / NEAR GRAND GULF

Home / MISSISSIPPI RIVER, NEAR GRAND GULF

Presbyterian church / RODNEY

A village pet, Mr. John Paul's Boy / RODNEY

Arlington / NATCHEZ

Home open to the public / DUNLEITH, NATCHEZ; THE FIRST GARDEN PILGRIMAGE

Presbyterian church / PORT GIBSON

Lilies on graves / RODNEY

The Mississippi River / NEAR NATCHEZ

Picnic at the ruins of Windsor—Hubert Creekmore, Eudora Welty, and Eileen McGrath / NEAR PORT GIBSON, 1954

Afterword / Welty Country

For countless generations the Old Natchez District had been on hold, waiting to connect with the artist. First came Audubon. Then, by the 1930s, when she went there with her camera and her inquiring eye, the landscape was ripe for Eudora Welty's searching encounter.

In the photographs she took there and in "Some Notes on River Country," she explores these lands known also as the Old Southwest, once America's riskiest far frontier. At once she seized it for her storytelling. "Some Notes on River Country" documents her discovery of this terrain and of "place," which Welty would come to recognize as the orienting spring of her fiction.

Rich in history, teeming with evocative folklore, "river country" comprises, now as then, a necklace of little Mississippi towns and hamlets between Vicksburg and Natchez. In the nineteenth century they sparkled brightly within a choking jungle of cedars, mosses, cane, live oaks, wild grape, and honeysuckle. Time and again, thwarting every human struggle to civilize it, the land reclaimed its own. Snaking alongside the hills and vales of this imposing setting was the great river with its drifting, wreathing bayous.

In the years before the Louisiana Purchase, in the years before this Mississippi territory was granted statehood, this raw place was the nation's far edge, as sinister as the impenetrable thickets beyond the wide river that formed its western border.

Welty's closeness to nature was expressed earliest in her writings about river country. In them the reader discerns her reverent, almost pantheistic interest in this life-giving, life-claiming terrain. Although her Jackson home is in central Mississippi, her work is so suffused with this landscape that it justifiably can be called Welty Country. Anyone wishing to know her early writings intimately should comprehend the spell that it cast over her and to discern how her experiences there were channeled through her fiction ever after.

"The cloak of vegetation," she writes in "Some Notes on River Country," ". . . has caught up this whole land for the third time, or the fourth, or the hundredth. . . . Here are nests for the birds and thrones for owls and trapezes for snakes, every kind of bower in the world."

Through this feral scene had wandered one of the most multifarious cohorts ever to enliven American history. Included among the various and assorted heroes and villains were the politically soured Aaron Burr and his co-conspirator Harmon Blennerhasset, the naturalist and painter John

James Audubon, the flatboatman Mike Fink, the thundering preacher Lorenzo Dow, the outlaw John Murrell, and the murderous brothers called Big Harp and Little Harp. Down the Natchez Trace had come the wagonloads of meandering pioneers from the Carolinas and the Tidewater country, ready to mingle with the plebeians and the planter aristocracy in a new land, but prey, all too often, to the lurking brigands along the trail.

Here and there in this motley wild, civility somehow blossomed.

Of even more momentous impact for Welty than the historical setting was the indelible identity of river country. Striking both the creative imagination and the intellect of this receptive romantic were its pulsating presence and its revelation that, no matter what the generations had imposed on its surface, place persisted as a steadily revealing essence connecting the land and its sensitive perceiver.

In a writer of Eudora Welty's feelings the discovery of river country and this "sense of place" was profound and transforming. It not only offered her rich resources that had never before been tapped but also bolstered and affirmed the approach she had been taking in her fiction—to write knowingly of an identifiable place without the baggage of local-color regionalists.

Although historians from Claiborne to Coates had described this fascinating land and its personages, no writer ever captured the magic as Welty did, and none has surpassed her in the attempt to bring it into literature. Like Willa Cather's *Death Comes for the Archbishop* and like Keats's "On First

Looking into Chapman's Homer," her river country essay and her novel *The Robber Bridegroom* are literary works that share an author's enormous joy of discovery. Welty did not restrain her desire to respond.

"I just sat down," she said, "and wrote *The Robber Bridegroom* in a great spurt of pleasure."[1]

"Some Notes on River Country" is both an idyllic travelogue and, unwittingly, Welty's intimate account of her creative impulse in performance. The essay seems an attempt at resolution, a settling down after the passionate elation of writing *The Robber Bridegroom*, her fantastical narrative in which this setting collided with her unstoppable urge to recount tales. However, although she tries in writing the essay to come back to earth, she soars anew.

"Why, just to write about what might happen along some little road like the Natchez Trace—which reaches so far into the past and has been the trail for so many kinds of people—is enough to keep you busy for life."[2]

Published two years after *The Robber Bridegroom*, "Some Notes on River Country" appeared in *Harper's Bazaar* in February 1944, when Welty was thirty-five and the author of two story collections. In the following decade she published "Place in Fiction" (1957), her credo of how a sure sense of place validates a writer's fiction as true. Place, she says in this essay, is "the named, identified, concrete, exact and exacting, and therefore credible, gathering spot of all that has been felt in the novel's progress."[3]

At the Windsor ruins / NEAR PORT GIBSON, 1954

"Fairy Tale of the Natchez Trace" (1975) is an account of writing *The Robber Bridegroom*, in which her heightened imagination dreamily commingles the Brothers Grimm, Mississippi history, and "the wild and romantic beauty of that place." She describes this wonder-filled novel as her "awakening to a dear native land and its own story of early life, made and offered by a novelist's imagination in exuberance and joy."[4]

In "Some Notes on River Country," place *then* and place *now* is her theme. Welty describes a long-familiar scene as freshly understood in the first encounter and in reflection. Her camera was seldom far from her side as she rambled. The photographs she took in river country draw on the same impulses that excited her imagination for story writing. These black-and-white images of ruins, old churches, mossy cedars, leaning fences, and Easter lilies festooning graves rimmed with brickbats reveal the persistence of place asserting its identity, of the land reclaiming itself as decay redeems the rough past from taming ways of civilization.

When did Welty first go to river country? Both *The Robber Bridegroom* and a clutch of her short stories—"A Worn Path" (1941), "Asphodel" (1942), "First Love" (1942), "A Still Moment" (1942), "Livvie" (1942), "At the Landing" (1943)—show the trail of her encounters along the Natchez Trace and at Windsor and Rodney. It is known that she had read Audubon's diaries, J. F. H. Claiborne's Mississippi narratives, and Robert M. Coates's *The Outlaw Years: The Land Pirates of the Natchez Trace* (1930) and wished to verify the history these told. She went to Grand Gulf in the 1930s, camera in hand. Along the primitive riverfront she met those men throwing knives at a target.

Who was with her when she took that picture?

"I went there alone in the family car," Welty recalled.

Of course there is an actual setting outside the frame of any photograph. A study of this shot causes one to imagine the identity of the photographer, a shy but stimulated stranger, a daring picture taker at risk just in being on the scene. Who are these men? An idle fisherman and his boys whiling away time by throwing knives? Some disagreeable confrontation might occur, for in this loveless, desolate spot a lone young woman artist has chanced upon them with her camera. Although the little boy in the picture softens the threatening edge, there is an awareness of female vulnerability in the presence of masculine force.

Yet no furor erupted. The men turned out to be affable country fellows, but from this, or from some such stirring encounter, Welty wrote "At the Landing," a wondrous strange story set in lonely Rodney's Landing.

An uneasy mood of loneliness and isolation also pervades Welty's story "Livvie." Its sequestered setting is a distance off the Old Natchez Trace. Longing for fulfillment, a vital young wife confined by an aged, dying husband steals away from his remote home place and meets a virile young lover "in the bursting light of spring."

River country, a source book for stories, continued to beckon to Welty. On one trip, she and a few friends enjoyed a picnic lunch on the former lawns of Windsor. This splendid mansion, which surfaces in Welty's story "Asphodel" and in *The Robber Bridegroom*, had burned in the 1890s and, from the imaginations of many who never saw Windsor before the fire, it continues to be touted as once having been the finest house in all the Mississippi Valley.

A favorite spot for excursions, Windsor was a site Welty shared with

Henry Miller beside the columns of Windsor / NEAR PORT GIBSON, 1940S

out-of-town guests. In the 1940s she and two safeguarding male chums entertained the author Henry Miller, notorious for his salacious prose and impropriety. While traveling about America, he had sallied down to Jackson at the recommendation of Welty's editor. In Welty's recollection of his stopover in Mississippi, Miller was mainly blasé and inattentive rather than the sexual gadabout portrayed in his steamy books. At Windsor she took a photograph of him standing as inert and passive as one of the columns. One is apt not only to recall the lecherous goat-man in "Asphodel" but also to wonder if Welty's subdued photographic image of Miller is on the same roll of film as her other shots of river country. Was Miller looking over her shoulder as she snapped Port Gibson's dramatic hand-topped church spire and as she photographed her own shadow streaming towards the ruined columns of Windsor?

Having witnessed the abiding spirit of place while on her early sojourns in river country, she said, "I have never seen . . . anything so mundane as ghosts." Yet in the 1950s when Welty took her friend the Irish writer Elizabeth Bowen to Natchez, a river-country ghost came forth to greet them. Early on a Sunday morning they strolled the grounds of opulent Longwood, the octagonal mansion left unfinished after war was declared and the Northern workers laid down their tools and departed for home.

"The groundskeeper asked us if we wanted a drink," Welty remembered. "We told him 'No thank you, we didn't believe so,' and he held up a tiny bottle about the size of a turpentine bottle. Later we mentioned this encounter and were told, 'Oh, no, you couldn't have met the groundskeeper. He died last week.'"

"Some Notes on River Country" focuses closely on Port Gibson (according to invading General Grant, "too pretty to burn"), on Grand Gulf (eroded nearly to oblivion by the ravenous river), and on Rodney's Landing (the river's forsaken relic). As Welty sees the present avatar of decay she imagines the past, especially in Rodney and in Grand Gulf. Her vision is of the lasting identity on the land as it passed, era upon era, from the indigenous peoples through the periods of Spanish, French, and British rule, through American dominion, and into the early twentieth century.

In its heyday Rodney had been a prospering river port, but at the times Welty went there it was far along into sorrowful decline. The town's name honored Thomas Rodney, appointed territorial judge by President Jefferson. He was a native of Delaware and a brother of Caesar Rodney, a signer of the Declaration of Independence.

After the Mississippi's nearby oxbow curve had shifted and closed, the capricious river forsook thriving, bustling Rodney and moved a few miles west. By the 1930s the population had fallen so far below the norm that the state legislature removed Rodney's status as a township and officially declared it to be a ghost town. While working as a WPA publicist, Welty learned of Rodney's predicament and was so eager to behold a ghost town that she made her initial trek there.

She describes Rodney as suspended between its hilltop graveyard and its often flooded bottomlands. Even more than majestic, much vaunted Natchez, it is tiny, forlorn Rodney in its romantic isolation that seizes Welty's especial attention. Both in her prose and in her photographs she muses over its deserted churches, the flood-streaked homes, and the burying ground on the bluff. These reveal how, in the grasp of decay, civility has become rustic. Both the face and the fact of this prove for Welty that place is like a smoldering fire that can flare or wane. Rodney's time has come and gone, but this land is destined to blaze again, yet in new attire. Whatever the vicissitudes, the remaining spark awaits ignition for the next phase. Welty the artist, happening to pass by, senses its flutter.

In her feeling portrait of the deserted village, she draws back the veil of the familiar to reveal a few lingering residents who still weave in and out of the shadows. One of the native spirits attesting to Rodney's sputtering past is the poignant imbecile who, without any sense of the ridiculous, introduced himself to Welty, not as "Mr. John Paul's *son*," but as "Mr. John Paul's Boy." (In the essay she applies a fictional touch by calling him "Mr. John *David's* Boy.") Although in his sixties, he remains a prattling child. In him she perceives an ancient archetype, the village "pet," a pathetic care that all the dwindling town looked after. He welcomed strangers like Welty, a cordial, passible visitor, and served them as a pestering guide.

"Wild wistaria hangs its flowers like flower-grapes above reach," Welty writes of the smothering scrim with which lovely nature covers the decay of river country. "All over the hills the beautiful white Cherokee Rose trails its glossy dark-green leaves and delicate luminous-white flowers."

This "sense of place," not a romantic evocation but an accommodation of the artist's feeling, is the stimulus that, as Welty often said, ignited her to write, for fiction is "bound up in the local." She does not disclose exactly from which side of the encounter the "sense of place" emanated. She leaves the matter blurred. Was "sense of place" nature's own essence? Was it the perceiver's feeling? Was it the shared, savored connection made during the exchange? Whatever she deemed it to be, its pulsating call to Welty never ceased.

—HUNTER COLE

1. *Conversations with Eudora Welty*, ed. Peggy Whitman Prenshaw (Jackson: University Press of Mississippi, 1984), p. 24.

2. Ibid., p. 5.

3. *The Eye of the Story* (New York: Random House, 1977), p. 122.

4. Ibid., p. 314.